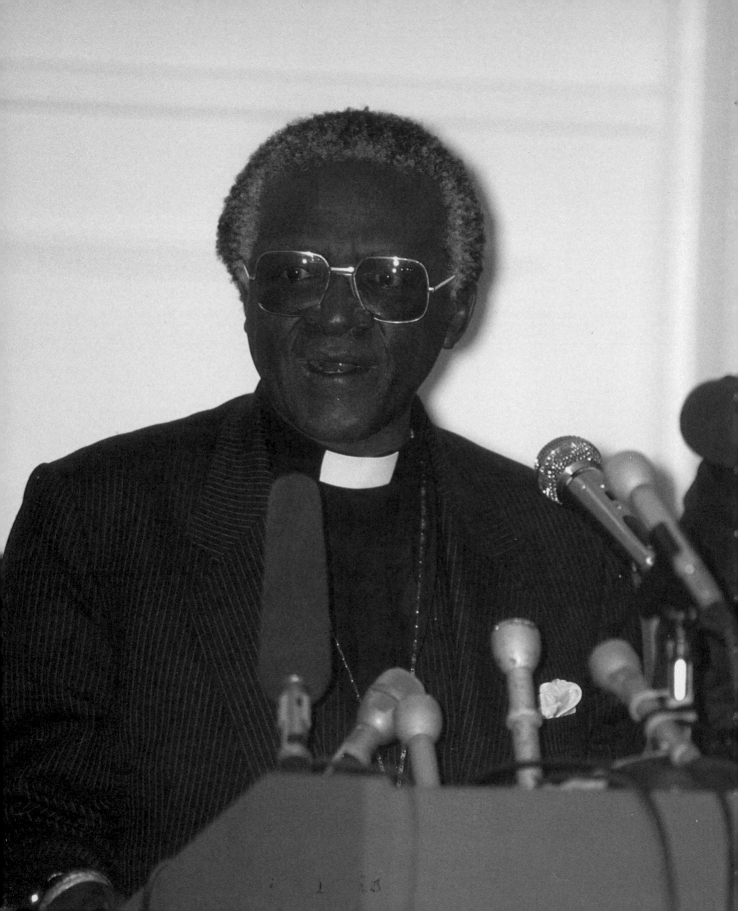

DESMOND TUTU
Bishop of Peace

By Carol Greene

CHILDRENS PRESS®
CHICAGO

Dedication
for Kwasi Thornell

Picture Acknowledgements

AP/Wide World—6, 8, 11 (top), 22, 23, 25, 29, 30, 31 (left)

Nawrocki Stock Photo:

© Ken Sexton—cover

© SISSAC—2

Reuters/Bettmann Newsphotos—26, 27, 28, 31 (right)

United Press International—11 (bottom), 12, 13, 15 (two photos), 17 (left), 19, 20 (two photos), 21

Horizon Graphics—17 (right)

Library of Congress Cataloging-in-Publication Data

Greene, Carol.

    Desmond Tutu, bishop of peace.

    Summary: Profiles the life of the South African bishop who has worked energetically and courageously to improve the lot of black people in South Africa.

    1. Tutu, Desmond—Juvenile literature. 2. Church of the Province of South Africa—Clergy—Biography—Juvenile literature. 3. Anglican Communion—South Africa— Clergy—Biography—Juvenile literature. [1. Tutu, Desmond. 2. Clergy. 3. South Africa— Biography] I. Title.

BX5700.6.Z8T874   1986   283'.3 [B] [92]   86-9582

ISBN 0-516-03634-3

DESMOND TUTU
Bishop of Peace

At a press conference, Bishop Tutu said he hoped the Nobel Peace Prize would "help focus the attention of the world" on South Africa's apartheid system.

Bishop Desmond Tutu knew it would be cold in Oslo, Norway that December day in 1984. But he did not know that he and his hosts would have to stand outdoors for ninety minutes.

He had come to this hall in Norway to receive the Nobel Peace Prize. Then, at the last moment, there was a bomb threat. Someone had threatened to blow up the hall and Bishop Tutu.

Desmond and Leah Tutu stand with Nobel officials on the stairs of Oslo University after the hall was cleared because of a bomb threat.

"This just shows how desperate our enemies have become," said Bishop Tutu.

Police searched every inch of the hall. They found no bombs. After the search everyone went back inside and Bishop Tutu received his Peace Prize. He was excited. But he was sad, too.

"There is no peace in South Africa," he said, "because there is no justice."

Bishop Tutu had spent many years working for justice and peace in South Africa. He had received awards and honorary degrees from all over the world for his work. But there was still so much to be done.

Desmond Mpilo Tutu was born on October 7, 1931. His father, Zachariah, taught in a Methodist school. His mother, Aletta, was a servant. The family lived in Klerksdorp, a gold-mining town in Transvaal, South Africa.

Baby Desmond was very weak. His family thought he might die. But his grandmother gave him a special middle name, Mpilo. In a Bantu language Mpilo means "life." Desmond lived.

As he grew, Desmond learned some hard things. He learned that although 70 percent of the people in South Africa were black they could not vote in national elections. They could not live or own land wherever they wanted to. They could not move when they wanted to. But the government could make them move at any time.

Desmond learned that white children got free lunches at school. They often threw them away. They liked their lunches from home better.

In 1960 this crowd gathered at Sharpeville, a black township south of Johannesburg. They were protesting a law that made all South African blacks over sixteen carry passbooks showing where they live and work. The government used such laws to keep blacks from coming freely into white-run cities. A few hours after this picture was taken, police arrived and opened fire. Sixty people were killed and hundreds injured.

Police examine the passbook of a black who is going to Johannesburg to work in the mines for six months. In 1986 the passbook law was changed.

This was the last day at a mission school for blacks. The government said blacks could not receive the same education as whites. The mission schools would not obey this rule. Instead, they closed down.

Black children did not get free lunches. Desmond watched them crowd around trash cans. They ate the lunches the white children threw away.

Ray Street is in the center of Sophiatown, the black shanty-town section of Johannesburg. In the background is the Church of Christ the King served by the fathers of the Anglican Community of the Resurrection.

When Desmond was twelve, his family moved to the big city of Johannesburg. There his mother worked as a cook in a missionary school for the blind. At the school Desmond saw people caring about and helping other people. That touched something deep inside him. Someday, he decided, he would help people, too.

13

One day Desmond was standing with his mother when a white man walked by. His name was Trevor Huddleston. He was an Anglican priest who worked in the black section of Johannesburg called Sophiatown.

Suddenly, Father Huddleston took off his hat as a sign of respect for Mrs. Tutu. Desmond could not believe his eyes. White men did not show respect that way in South Africa—not for poor black working women.

Desmond had learned something new. He did not have to feel bad about being black. Black people were just as good as white people.

Blacks who worked in Johannesburg once lived in overcrowded shacks in Sophiatown (above). As part of their apartheid policy, the government tore down the slums and built new houses (below) out in bare country. These new houses were cleaner. But now blacks had to travel for hours on slow buses to and from work.

In 1945, Desmond went to Madibane High School. To earn extra money, he sold peanuts at train stations and caddied at a golf course. He knew what he wanted to do when he finished school. He wanted to become a doctor.

But medical school cost too much. So Desmond went to Pretoria Bantu Normal College. He would be a teacher instead.

About that time, he became ill with tuberculosis. He had to stay in the hospital for twenty months. What would happen to his education now? he wondered.

Every day Father Huddleston came to see him. He brought him books and talked with him. Desmond never

To protest higher fares, blacks boycotted the buses in 1957.
They used other types of transportation, including foot power.

gave up hope. In fact, *he* cheered up
Father Huddleston.

By 1954, Desmond was teaching at
Madibane High School. Then he
taught at Munsieville High School in
Krugersdorp. In 1955, he married
Leah Nomalizo. They had four
children, three girls and a boy. They
named the boy Trevor after Father
Huddleston.

Then, in 1957, the government said black students could no longer receive the same education as white students. They must get a "Bantu education." Many teachers felt this was wrong. They quit their jobs in protest. Desmond Tutu was one of them.

Again his life changed. He began studying to become a priest in the Anglican church. In 1961, he was ordained.

At first Father Tutu served a church in South Africa. Then, in 1962, he moved his family to England. There he studied at King's College, London, and worked in different churches.

In 1967, the Tutus returned to South Africa. Father Tutu taught, first at Federal Theological Seminary,

To many, Johannesburg was the "Golden City." Its wealth, controlled by the whites, was built on gold, diamonds, and uranium taken from its nearby mines.

then at the National University of Lesotho. In 1972, he went back to England to work with scholarships for the World Council of Churches.

But in 1975, Father Tutu was chosen Anglican Dean of Johannesburg. That made him the first black dean in the Anglican church.

Rioters burn a government bus during the second day of demonstrations in Soweto Township, fifteen miles south of Johannesburg. The blacks were protesting the government's 1957 decision to force black schools to teach the Dutch-based Afrikaans language.

Police stand over the body of a white person killed in the Soweto riots. Six people died and more than forty people were injured in the disturbance.

In 1977 black students at Meadowland School in Soweto burned their schoolbooks to protest the government's Afrikaans policy. The police used tear gas to break up the more than six thousand demonstrators.

As dean, he tried to tell the South African government how unfairly they were treating black people. Some, he said, were held in prison for long periods without being charged. Dean Tutu wanted both sides to settle their problems peacefully. But he knew that many young blacks were angry. Anything might happen.

The government ignored him. On June 16, 1976, riots broke out in the Soweto area. Six hundred black people were shot and killed.

That same year, Desmond Tutu became Bishop of Lesotho. Lesotho is an independent kingdom in the middle of South Africa. Bishop Tutu could have become a citizen there.

But he didn't. He loved his

Both black and white students protested apartheid in downtown Johannesburg. Here they are running from a police attack.

A student is detained by police during a demonstration.

beautiful South Africa, even though she hurt him by treating black people so badly.

In 1978, Bishop Tutu became Secretary General of the South African Council of Churches. This group worked hard to help people in need. The government did not like the way they helped political prisoners.

The government did not like what Bishop Tutu did in 1979, either. Blacks were being moved from cities to poor tribal lands. Bishop Tutu said they were starving because of the government.

Soon he began asking the United States and countries in Europe to stop trading with South Africa. If South Africa lost money, the policies toward blacks might be changed.

To punish him, the government took away Bishop Tutu's passport. They would not let him go to New York City to get an honorary degree from Columbia University. So the president of Columbia flew to South Africa to present the degree. He called Bishop Tutu "a symbol of hope for a unified Africa."

Bishop Desmond Tutu displays his gold medal after accepting the 1984 Nobel Peace Prize in Oslo. Egil Aarvik, right, chairman of the Nobel Peace Prize committee, holds his Nobel Diploma.

By 1984, the bishop was able to travel to General Theological Seminary in New York. There, on October 16, he heard that he had been chosen to receive the Nobel Peace Prize. The citation with the award praised all South African blacks who had worked for peaceful change.

"Hey, we are winning!" said Bishop Tutu. "Justice is going to win." He also said he would use

Black mourners chanted slogans at the funeral of a riot victim. They carried a banner against apartheid. Later, police broke up the group and took the banner.

much of the $193,000 cash prize for scholarships for poor South African blacks.

In November of 1984, he became Bishop of Johannesburg and quit his job with the South African Council of Churches. Meanwhile, riots, boycotts, and protests went on. Again and again Bishop Tutu begged both sides to work together peacefully.

On August 6, 1985, he watched as angry government police and blacks faced each other. The blacks were on their way to a funeral. The police thought they would riot.

Quietly, Bishop Tutu suggested that the police get buses for the blacks. These could take them where they were going and there would be no riot.

Blacks were getting ready to bury another riot victim when these armed security forces moved in.

All too often the funerals of blacks have turned into violent anti-government demonstrations. Since 1984 more than 1,500 people—most of them black—have been killed in riots.

The police agreed and the funeral took place peacefully.

Another time, the bishop saw a group of blacks trying to stone a policeman to death. He threw his own body across the policeman's and saved his life.

Bishop Tutu had spoken many words about his belief in peaceful change for South Africa. He had written two books, *Crying in the Wilderness* and *Hope and Suffering*.

But words would not have helped that policeman. So Bishop Tutu risked his life instead.

Bishop Desmond Tutu is a small man. He loves to read, jog, listen to music, and laugh. He loves to tell stories to the people in his churches. His favorite is the biblical story of the Exodus. In that story, God freed His people who were slaves in Egypt.

Bishop Tutu waded into an angry crowd of blacks who were attacking a suspected police informant. Tutu shouted at the mob to stop the beating. He ordered the man carried to a nearby car. "Tutu definitely saved the man's life," said a reporter.

Bishop Tutu believes that God wants people to be free today, too. He says that Jesus came to earth to free people, *all* people, no matter what color they are. That, says Bishop Tutu, is why he works so hard to help black people in South Africa.

In 1986 Coretta Scott King, left, awarded Bishop Tutu the Martin Luther King Peace Award. Christine King Farris, center, the sister of Martin Luther King, and Tutu's daughter Mpho, right, also took part in the ceremony held in the Ebenezer Baptist Church in Atlanta, Georgia.

Bishop Tutu speaks against apartheid whenever and wherever he can.

It is not an easy job—or a safe one. But Bishop Tutu says he is not afraid. He says the government cannot stop him because he is doing what God wants him to do.

"I cannot help it," he wrote. "When I see injustice, I cannot keep quiet....The most awful thing that they can do is to kill me, and death is not the worst thing that could happen to a Christian."

31

DESMOND MPILO TUTU

TIMELINE

1931	October 7—Born in Klerksdorp, Transvaal, South Africa, to Zachariah and Aletta Tutu
1950	Was graduated from Madibane High School, Johannesburg
1953	Received Teacher's Diploma from Pretoria Bantu Normal College
1954	Received Bachelor of Arts degree from University of South Africa
1954-55	Taught at Madibane High School
1955	Married Leah Nomalizo
1955-57	Taught at Munsieville High School, Krugersdorp
1958-60	Studied at St. Peter's Theological Seminary, Johannesburg
1961	Became an ordained priest in the Anglican church
1965	Received Bachelor of Divinity degree, King's College, London, England
1966	Received Master of Theology degree, King's College, London, England
1967-69	Taught at Federal Theological Seminary, South Africa
1969-71	Taught at National University of Lesotho
1972-75	Worked as Associate Director of the Theological Education Fund, England
1975	Became Anglican Dean of Johannesburg
1976	Became Bishop of Lesotho
1978-84	Worked as Secretary General of the South African Council of Churches
1982	Received honorary Doctor of Sacred Theology degree from Columbia University
1984	Received the Nobel Peace Prize; became Bishop of Johannesburg
1986	Became Anglican Archbishop of Capetown

ABOUT THE AUTHOR

CAROL GREENE has degrees in English Literature and Musicology. She has worked in international exchange programs, as an editor, and as a teacher. She now lives in St. Louis, Missouri and writes full time. She has published over fifty books—most of them for children. Other Childrens Press biographies by Ms. Greene include *Sandra Day O'Connor, Mother Teresa, Indira Nehru Gandhi,* and *Diana, Princess of Wales* in the Picture-Story Biographies series, and *Louisa May Alcott, Marie Curie, Thomas Alva Edison,* and *Hans Christian Andersen* in the People of Distinction series.